HISTORICAL PERSPECTIVES
In Their Own Words

I0811637

# The Words of NEIL ARMSTRONG

Jagger Youssef

PowerKiDS press

Published in 2023 by The Rosen Publishing Group, Inc.
2544 Clinton Street, Buffalo, NY 14224

Copyright © 2023 by The Rosen Publishing Group, Inc.

All rights reserved. No part of this book may be reproduced in any form without permission in writing from the publisher, except by a reviewer.

Portions of this work were originally authored by Ryan Nagelhout and published as *Neil Armstrong in His Own Words*. All new material in this edition authored by Jagger Youssef.

Editor: Therese Shea
Book Design: Michael Flynn

Photo Credits: Cover https://commons.wikimedia.org/wiki/File:Astronaut_Neil_A._Armstrong_(1964).jpg; (series background) merrymuuu/Shutterstock.com; (fact box) Miloje/Shutterstock.com; p. 5 https://commons.wikimedia.org/wiki/File:Neil_Armstrong_pose.jpg; p. 7 Todd Pettibone/Shutterstock.com; p. 8 https://commons.wikimedia.org/wiki/File:Aeronca_7ac_champion_g-bpfm_1946_arp.jpg; p. 9 https://commons.wikimedia.org/wiki/File:Blume_High_School,_southeastern_angle.jpg; p. 11 https://commons.wikimedia.org/wiki/File:Pilot_Neil_Armstrong_and_X-15_-1_-_GPN-2000-000121.jpg; p. 13 https://commons.wikimedia.org/wiki/File:Neil_Armstrong_in_Gemini_G-2C_training_suit.jpg; p. 15 (launch) https://commons.wikimedia.org/wiki/File:Gemini_8_launch.jpg; p. 15 (Scott and Armstrong) Portrait of the Gemini 8 prime crew.jpg; p. 17 https://commons.wikimedia.org/wiki/File:Armstrong_and_Scott_with_Hatches_Open_-_GPN-2000-001413.jpg; p. 19 https://commons.wikimedia.org/wiki/File:Apollo_11_LLRV_1.jpg; p. 20 https://en.wikipedia.org/wiki/Apollo_11#/media/File:Apollo_11_Crew.jpg; p. 21 https://en.wikipedia.org/wiki/File:Apollo_11_Launch_-_GPN-2000-000630.jpg; p. 23 https://commons.wikimedia.org/wiki/File:Apollo_11_Lunar_Module_Eagle_in_landing_configuration_in_lunar_orbit_from_the_Command_and_Service_Module_Columbia.jpg; p. 24 https://en.wikipedia.org/wiki/Lunar_soil#/media/File:Apollo_11_bootprint.jpg; p. 25 https://en.wikipedia.org/wiki/File:Buzz_salutes_the_U.S._Flag.jpg; p. 27 (Nixon and crew) https://commons.wikimedia.org/wiki/File:President_Nixon_welcomes_the_Apollo_11_astronauts_aboard_the_U.S.S._Hornet.jpg; p. 27 (lunar module in space) https://commons.wikimedia.org/wiki/File:Apollo_11_lunar_module.jpg.

**Library of Congress Cataloging-in-Publication Data**

Names: Youssef, Jagger, author.
Title: The words of Neil Armstrong / Jagger Youssef.
Description: New York : PowerKids Press, [2023] | Series: Historical perspectives: in their own words | Includes index.
Identifiers: LCCN 2022028032 (print) | LCCN 2022028033 (ebook) | ISBN 9781642824704 (library binding) | ISBN 9781642824681 (paperback) | ISBN 9781642824711 (ebook)
Subjects: LCSH: Armstrong, Neil, 1930-2012--Juvenile literature. | Project Apollo (U.S.)--Juvenile literature. | Astronauts--United States--Biography--Juvenile literature. | Space flight to the moon--History--Juvenile literature.
Classification: LCC TL789.85.A75 Y68 2023 (print) | LCC TL789.85.A75 (ebook) | DDC 629.450092 [B]--dc23/eng/20220713
LC record available at https://lccn.loc.gov/2022028032
LC ebook record available at https://lccn.loc.gov/2022028033

Manufactured in the United States of America

Some of the images in this book illustrate individuals who are models. The depictions do not imply actual situations or events.

CPSIA Compliance Information: Batch #CWPK23. For further information contact Rosen Publishing at 1-800-237-9932.

Find us on

# CONTENTS

# DESTINED FOR SPACE

Neil Armstrong is perhaps the most famous figure of space exploration. Space-science fans learn early that Armstrong was the first human to walk on the moon, as part of the Apollo 11 mission. Though he found fame through his work, he was a quiet and humble person and didn't like the spotlight.

Armstrong seemed destined for great things even in childhood. He was focused on achieving his goals. As a young man, he became an Eagle Scout, the highest rank in the Boy Scouts. He went on to pursue a career in the air, becoming a navy pilot and an astronaut. He later became a professor of **aerospace** engineering. Neil Armstrong is remembered and honored today as an American hero.

## LOOKING BACK

Neil Armstrong once said, "I believe that every human has a finite [set] number of heartbeats. I don't intend to waste any of mine."

# A Full Life of Fireworks

In 2005, Neil Armstrong said, "I guess we all like to be recognized not for one piece of fireworks, but for the **ledger** of our daily work." Armstrong was proud of his many accomplishments, not just the journey to the moon and back. In this book, you'll learn more about his life through his own words, including those famous words he spoke while taking his most momentous steps, onto the moon.

After the Apollo 11 mission, Neil Armstrong became one of the most famous people on Earth.

# INTRO TO AVIATION

Neil Armstrong was born August 5, 1930, on his grandparents' farm near Wapakoneta, Ohio. His parents, Stephen and Viola, had two other children: a daughter named June and a son named Dean. Because of Stephen's job with the state of Ohio, the Armstrong family relocated a lot when Neil was young.

Neil became interested in aviation, or the design and use of aircraft, when he was just a child. "I must have been a **staunch** aviation fan before I was even **conscious** of it," Armstrong recalled. At 2 years old, he accompanied his father to the National Air Races in Cleveland, Ohio. The planes amazed young Neil. When he was about 6, his father took him on his first airplane ride, in a Ford Trimotor.

## LOOKING BACK

The Ford Trimotor plane was made from 1925 to 1933. Only 199 were built.

## The Ford Trimotor

Stephen Armstrong recognized and encouraged young Neil's interest in airplanes. Neil's first flight was in a Ford Trimotor plane nicknamed the "Tin Goose." Neil and Stephen boarded the plane in Warren, Ohio. "We were supposed to be at church, I think," Armstrong later said. "But we sneaked off and later my mother caught us, just because of the guilty, and probably excited, looks on our faces."

This is a version of the airplane in which Neil Armstrong took his first flight, a Ford Trimotor.

Neil Armstrong maintained his enthusiasm for flight as he got older. "*By the time I was nine, I was building model airplanes,*" he said. "*They had become, I suppose, almost an **obsession** with me.*" He built a homemade wind tunnel in his basement, which he used to conduct experiments with his model planes. He read books and magazines on aviation too.

Armstrong began taking flying lessons when he was 15. He worked jobs at the airport and around his hometown, Wapakoneta, to pay for the lessons, which taught him to fly an Aeronca Champion plane. Lessons were $9 an hour in 1945—about $140 in today's money. Armstrong got his pilot's license when he was 16. He could legally fly a plane before he could drive a car!

Aeronca Champion plane

## The Navy and the War

Armstrong got a scholarship to attend college through service with the U.S. Navy. He went to Purdue University to study aeronautical engineering. In 1949, the navy called him to active service. He was stationed aboard the USS *Essex* aircraft carrier and flew 78 combat missions during the Korean War (1950–1953). On one mission, he had to use a parachute to escape a damaged plane. He received three medals for his military service.

### LOOKING BACK

Armstrong later received his master's degree in aerospace engineering from the University of Southern California in 1970.

Armstrong graduated from Blume High School in Wapakoneta, Ohio, in 1947.

# ENGINEER AT WORK

After his service in the Korean War, Armstrong went back to Purdue University and graduated in 1955. He began working as an engineer and test pilot for NACA (National Advisory Committee for Aeronautics) at the Lewis Flight Propulsion Laboratories in Cleveland, Ohio. He was soon transferred to the NACA High Speed Flight Station at Edwards Air Force Base in California.

Armstrong said this work helped him as an astronaut later in his life. "Our principal responsibility was engineering work. We did not do a lot of flying," Armstrong wrote in 1970. "It was program development, looking at the problems of flight. It was a wonderful time period, and it was very satisfying work, particularly when you found a solution."

## LOOKING BACK

Astronaut Michael Collins later wrote that Armstrong was "the very best [X-15 pilot] when it came to understanding the machine's design and how it operated."

# A Hypersonic Ride

The North American X-15 rocket-powered aircraft was a hypersonic research jet. That means it could go at least five times the speed of sound. Three rocket-powered X-15 jets flew 199 times between 1959 and 1968. The X-15 was attached to a B-52 bomber plane, then released in the air at a height of 45,000 feet (13,716 m) at around 500 miles (805 km) per hour. Armstrong flew the X-15 seven times, once covering 350 miles (563 km) in 12 minutes!

Armstrong flew a number of superfast test planes in the late 1950s and early 1960s, including the X-1B and the X-15.

# ENTER NASA

On October 4, 1957, the **Soviet Union** launched Sputnik I into orbit around Earth. The basketball-sized Sputnik was the world's first artificial, or human-made, **satellite**. The "Space Race" had begun. In 1958, the U.S. government formed NASA (National Aeronautics and Space Administration) in an effort to make the United States first in manned space flight. It picked seven test pilots in 1959 to be the first astronauts. However, Soviet astronaut, or cosmonaut, Yuri Gagarin went into orbit first, in 1961.

Neil Armstrong was one of nine astronauts NASA selected in its second class, in 1962. That same year, President John F. Kennedy gave an inspiring speech in which he declared the United States would send a mission to the moon by the end of the decade.

## LOOKING BACK

President Kennedy announced, "We choose to go to the moon in this decade and do . . . other things, not because they are easy, but because they are hard."

# Comfortable Up There

Neil Armstrong had experienced the dangers of military test planes. He thought spacecraft were safer. "I always felt that the risks we had in the space side of the program were probably less than we had back in flying at Edwards or the general flight-test community," Armstrong said. "That isn't to say that we didn't expect risks in the space program. But we felt pretty comfortable."

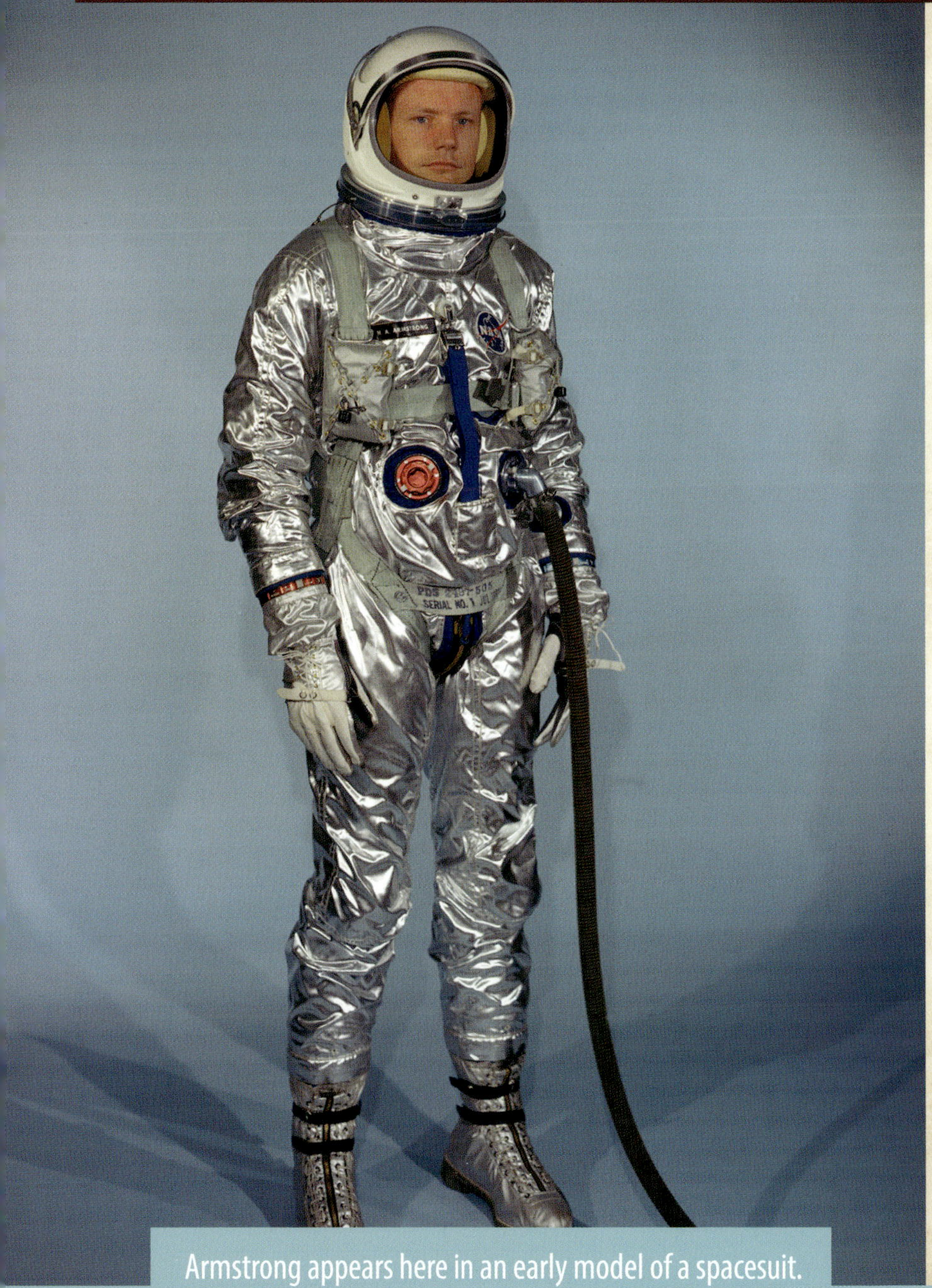

Armstrong appears here in an early model of a spacesuit.

# "THE BRIDGE TO THE MOON"

NASA called its Gemini space program "the bridge to the moon." The Gemini program had several goals, among them to test how astronauts could survive in space for a longer period, how spacecraft could dock in orbit, and how craft could reenter Earth's atmosphere safely. The first manned mission, Gemini 3, took place in 1965. Each mission was designed to build on what NASA scientists and astronauts learned on previous missions, slowly figuring out how to get to the moon and back.

Armstrong was picked as the command pilot for Gemini 8, along with pilot Dave Scott. The two were to leave Earth's atmosphere and dock with an unmanned craft called the Agena. A spacewalk was also planned for the mission, which launched on March 16, 1966.

## LOOKING BACK

Armstrong resigned from the U.S. Navy Reserve in 1960. The Gemini 8 mission of 1966 became the first time an American **civilian** entered orbit.

# Gemini and Titan

Spacecraft need a certain amount of **thrust** to escape Earth's gravity. For the Gemini 8 spacecraft, the thrust was provided by a giant rocket called a Titan II. The Titan had two parts, called stages. Each had its own engine. When the rocket's fuel was consumed, the Titan II fell away from the rest of the craft as it entered space. Armstrong reported the ride was smooth. "The second stage is a real good machine," he said a few minutes into the flight.

This photo shows Gemini 8's launch from Cape Canaveral, Florida (then called Cape Kennedy).

When Gemini 8 was in orbit, the crew got their first look at Earth. "That's fantastic!" Armstrong exclaimed. They got to work docking. Over the course of six hours, they made nine **maneuvers** to dock with the Agena. It was the first time two ships had docked in space.

Armstrong was thrilled. "That's just unbelievable!" he said as they moved within 900 feet (274 m) of the Agena. "Unbelievable! I can't believe it!"

Scott congratulated Armstrong on the docking: "Outstanding job, Coach!" Armstrong was quick to point out both astronauts had made it happen. "It takes two to tango," he replied.

But about 27 minutes after docking with the Agena, the two crafts began tumbling out of control. Armstrong had to act quickly to save the mission—and their lives.

## LOOKING BACK

When connected with the Agena, the Gemini craft pitched and yawed. A pitch motion is an up-and-down movement of the nose of an aircraft. Yaw is side-to-side movement of the nose.

## Quick Thinking

With the spacecraft starting to roll, about once per second, Armstrong quickly disconnected from the Agena and tried to regain control of the ship. He used all 16 reentry control system thrusters meant for returning to Earth, which stopped the craft's spin. But the move used 75 percent of the Gemini's reentry fuel. The crew had to cut the mission short and head back to Earth. The craft splashed safely into the Pacific Ocean to complete the mission.

Armstrong (right) and Scott are pictured here in Gemini 8, along with rescue crew, in the western Pacific Ocean.

# THE APOLLO PROGRAM

The Apollo program was NASA's third spaceflight program and was focused on fulfilling the promise of President Kennedy's 1961 speech. After his success in the Gemini 8 mission, Armstrong trained the next two years with the Apollo program. He was backup commander of Apollo 8, which sent the first craft to orbit the moon in December 1968.

Six months later, the Apollo 10 mission came within 47,000 feet (14 km) of the moon's surface. The mission was called the "dress rehearsal," or the final test, for a moon landing. Armstrong was selected as commander of the next mission, called Apollo 11. Michael Collins was chosen to be command **module** pilot, and Edwin "Buzz" Aldrin was named lunar module pilot.

## LOOKING BACK

Apollo 1's first mission ended in tragedy in 1967. A cabin fire during a launch test killed the three crew members: Gus Grissom, Ed White, and Roger B. Chaffee.

## Crash Landing

While training for Apollo 11 in 1968, Armstrong crashed a lunar landing research vehicle (LLRV) while testing it at Ellington Air Force Base near Houston, Texas. The vehicle's controls malfunctioned, and he was forced to eject from the pilot's seat. "I got up and walked away after I landed," Armstrong later said. "The only damage to me was that I bit my tongue." It was reported that if he had ejected a second later, his parachute wouldn't have worked.

This photo shows Neil Armstrong parachuting down, while his LLRV is in flames on the ground.

# LIFT OFF

On July 16, 1969, Apollo 11 launched from Kennedy Space Center in Florida. A three-stage Saturn V rocket drove the spacecraft out of Earth's atmosphere. It entered orbit about 12 minutes after launch. The rocket's third stage fired to head the craft toward the moon at a speed of 24,200 miles (38,946 km) per hour. After the stages detached, the remaining parts of the spacecraft were the command and service module, called *Columbia*, and the lunar module, called *Eagle*. They entered the moon's orbit on July 19.

On July 20, Armstrong and Buzz Aldrin entered *Eagle*, leaving Collins in *Columbia*, and prepared to land. "Man, this is really something; you ought to look at this," Armstrong said, amazed at the moon's craters and mountains.

## Just One Shot

Of all the challenges of the Apollo 11 mission, Armstrong was most worried about the landing. He thought there was a 50–50 chance that they wouldn't be able to pull it off. He and Aldrin had just 12 minutes to bring *Eagle* from 50,000 feet (15 km) above the moon to the surface safely—even though the craft would be traveling thousands of miles per hour. And there was only enough fuel for one landing attempt.

**LOOKING BACK**

After *Eagle* separated from *Columbia*, Armstrong said, "The *Eagle* has wings!"

Millions of people watched the launch from the surrounding area and on television.

# LUNAR LANDING

As *Eagle* made its descent, Armstrong and Aldrin realized they were traveling too fast and wouldn't land where they were supposed to. Suddenly, computer alarms went off—and neither astronaut knew what the alarm codes meant. The mission control center in Houston, Texas, said they meant that the computer was having trouble completing its tasks, but the mission could continue.

Armstrong took over piloting from the computer and found a flat surface. Despite blowing moon dust making the descent more difficult, he brought down the module gently and said the famous words: "Houston, Tranquility Base here. The *Eagle* has landed."

Armstrong was overjoyed. He later said, "That was the emotional high. And the business of getting down the ladder to me was much less significant."

## LOOKING BACK

The *Eagle* module landed on the moon with only 15 to 20 seconds of fuel remaining.

## A Sacrifice Avoided

If Armstrong and Aldrin had taken too long to land, they might not have had enough fuel to leave. U.S. president Richard Nixon had a speech ready in case something went wrong: "Fate has ordained that the men who went to the moon to explore in peace will stay on the moon to rest in peace. These brave men, Neil Armstrong and Edwin Aldrin, know that there is no hope for their recovery. But they also know that there is hope for mankind in their sacrifice."

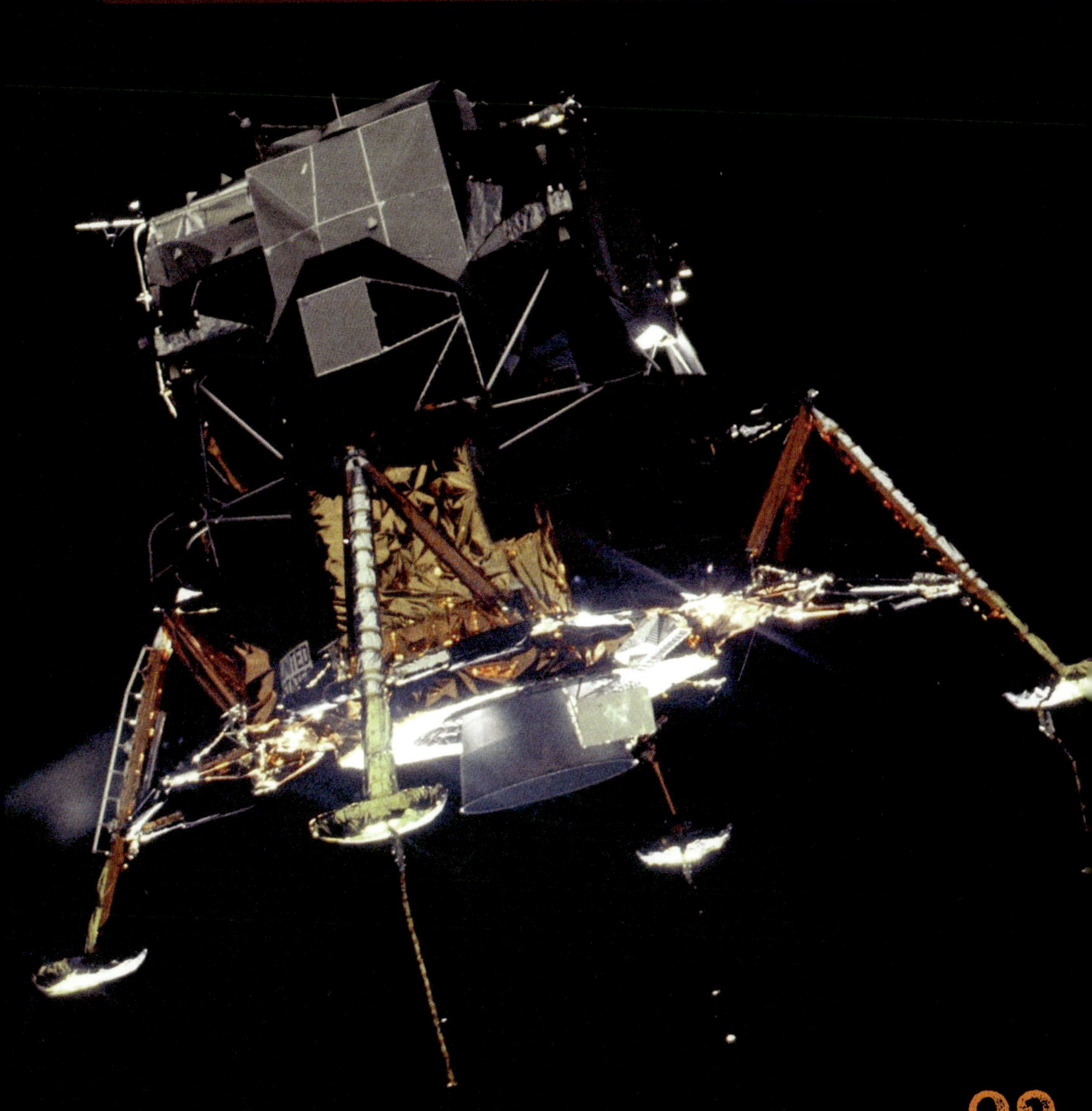

This is a photo of *Eagle* in lunar orbit, taken from *Columbia*.

Several hours after the lunar landing, Neil Armstrong got ready to climb down a ladder onto the moon's surface. A TV camera was set up for viewers back on Earth. About 110 hours into the mission, Neil Armstrong became the first person to walk on the moon. About 600 million people heard Armstrong say his most famous words: "*That's one small step for man, one giant leap for mankind.*" Aldrin followed Armstrong about 20 minutes later. He called the moon's rocky surface "*magnificent* ***desolation***."

The matter that covers the moon's surface, mostly a gray soil, is called lunar regolith. Armstrong described it: "*The surface is fine and powdery. I can kick it up loosely with my toe. It does adhere in fine layers, like powdered charcoal, to the sole and sides of my boots.*"

## LOOKING BACK

Armstrong and Aldrin tested the best way to walk on the moon. They "loped." "In loping," said Armstrong, "you leave the ground with both feet and come down with one foot in a normal running fashion."

## One Small Step for . . . ?

Armstrong later said he meant to say, "That's one small step for a man . . ." It's possible that he did and the transmission equipment didn't pick it up. Armstrong's brother Dean said the quote wasn't made up on the spot. He said Neil had asked for his opinion about it before the mission. However, others say Neil told them he thought of it just as he was preparing for that famous step.

Moon dust got everywhere. It covered spacesuits, gear, and other objects that came back to Earth from the mission.

# LUNAR EXPLORATION

Armstrong and Aldrin spent 21 hours and 36 minutes on the moon—about 2 1/2 hours of this time was exploring its surface. They performed scientific experiments, collected almost 50 pounds (23 kg) of surface samples, and took photographs. They also planted an American flag. They traveled about 3,300 feet (1 km) during their moonwalk, but there wasn't enough time to explore everything.

"There were a lot of interesting areas within 500 feet or so to go and look at if we had had the time," Armstrong said. "It would have been interesting to take that time and go out and inspect them closely and get some pictures, but that was a luxury we didn't have."

## LOOKING BACK

Before they left the moon's surface, Armstrong and Aldrin discovered the switch to turn *Eagle's* ascent engine on was broken. The astronauts fixed it with a pen!

# The Way Back

On July 21, the *Eagle* lunar module lifted off the moon's surface and docked with the command module *Columbia*. The lunar module was left in orbit. Then, *Columbia*, with all three astronauts back on it, began the return trip to Earth. The crew had few problems on their return. They splashed down in the Pacific Ocean on July 24, 1969. They were **quarantined** for 21 days to make sure they didn't return with a lunar sickness.

President Richard Nixon visits the quarantined astronauts

Armstrong credited others for the mission's success: "We would like to give special thanks to all those Americans who built the spacecraft; who did the construction, design, the tests, and put their hearts and all their abilities into those craft."

# AFTER SPACE

The Apollo 11 astronauts returned to celebrations, including parades and a world tour. Neil Armstrong said he didn't plan to go back into space. He worked at NASA until 1971. He went on to teach engineering at the University of Cincinnati until 1979 and lived on a farm. He also worked for various companies and government **commissions**. But for the most part, he led the quiet life that he wanted. He died in Ohio on August 25, 2012. A few weeks later, he was buried at sea in the Atlantic Ocean.

Armstrong's family said he was a "**reluctant** American hero [who had] served his nation proudly, as a navy fighter pilot, test pilot, and astronaut." They asked that his life be a reminder to young people to work hard to achieve their dreams.

## LOOKING BACK

Neil Armstrong, Buzz Aldrin, and Michael Collins were each awarded the Presidential Medal of Freedom, the highest award a U.S. civilian can be given.

## Fighting for NASA

Armstrong continued to speak on behalf of funding for NASA missions and encourage further space explorations. "I fully expected that, by the end of the century, we would have achieved substantially more than we actually did," he said. The last manned mission to the moon was Apollo 17 in 1972. NASA has planned the next moon landing for 2025.

## A Timeline of Neil Armstrong's Life

**1930** Neil Alden Armstrong is born August 5 near Wapakoneta, Ohio.

**1936** He takes his first flight.

**1946** He receives his pilot's license at age 16.

**1947** He begins to attend Purdue University.

**1949** The U.S. Navy calls Armstrong to active service. He went on to fly combat missions in the Korean War.

**1955** Armstrong graduates from Purdue with a degree in aeronautical engineering.
He begins working as a test pilot for the National Advisory Committee for Aeronautics.

**1962** Armstrong is chosen to be a NASA astronaut.

**1966** He is command pilot of Gemini 8.

**1969** He is mission commander of Apollo 11, during which he walks on the moon.

**1971** Armstrong resigns from NASA.
He begins to teach at the University of Cincinnati.

**1985** Armstrong serves on the National Commission on Space.

**2012** Armstrong dies on August 25 in Cincinnati, Ohio.

# GLOSSARY

**aerospace:** Having to do with Earth's atmosphere and the space beyond it.

**civilian:** A person not on active duty in the military.

**commission:** A group of people given power to carry out a task.

**conscious:** Aware of something.

**desolation:** Barren wasteland.

**ledger:** A book that a company uses to record information about the money it has paid and received.

**maneuver:** A planned movement.

**module:** A part of a space vehicle that can work alone.

**obsession:** Someone or something that a person thinks about constantly or frequently.

**quarantine:** To keep something away from the public to stop the spread of disease.

**reluctant:** Feeling unwilling.

**satellite:** A machine sent into space that moves around Earth, the moon, the sun, or a planet to complete scientific research or a type of communication.

**Soviet Union:** A former communist country that stretched from eastern Europe to Asia and was also known as the USSR.

**staunch:** Very devoted or loyal.

**thrust:** The force needed by an aircraft to overcome the resistance of air.

# FOR MORE INFORMATION

## Books


Buckley, James, Jr. *Neil Armstrong: First Man on the Moon!* San Diego, CA: Portable Press, 2021.

Howard, Martin. *The Extraordinary Life of Neil Armstrong.* Tulsa, OK: Kane Miller, 2020.

Page, Nathan. *Who Was the First Man on the Moon? Neil Armstrong.* New York, NY: Penguin Workshop, 2022.


## Websites

**Apollo 11 Mission Overview**
*www.nasa.gov/mission_pages/apollo/missions/apollo11.html*
Read about the mission, according to NASA.

**Biography of Neil Armstrong**
*www.nasa.gov/centers/glenn/about/bios/neilabio.html*
Read more about the many honors Armstrong received because of his life and work.

**Neil Armstrong's First Steps on the Moon**
*thekidshouldseethis.com/post/apollo-11-moon-nasa-first-steps*
Check out video of this historic event.


**Publisher's note to educators and parents:** Our editors have carefully reviewed these websites to ensure that they are suitable for students. Many websites change frequently, however, and we cannot guarantee that a site's future contents will continue to meet our high standards of quality and educational value. Be advised that students should be closely supervised whenever they access the internet.

# INDEX